EDGE

BY ADAM STONE

TORQUE™

BELLWETHER MEDIA · MINNEAPOLIS, MN

Are you ready to take it to the extreme?
Torque books thrust you into the action-packed world
of sports, vehicles, mystery, and adventure. These books
may include dirt, smoke, fire, and dangerous stunts.
WARNING: read at your own risk.

Library of Congress Cataloging-in-Publication Data

Stone, Adam.
 Edge / by Adam Stone.
   p. cm. -- (Torque: pro wrestling champions)
 Includes bibliographical references and index.
 Summary: "Engaging images accompany information about Edge. The combination of high-interest
subject matter and light text is intended for students in grades 3 through 7"--Provided by publisher.
 ISBN 978-1-60014-685-0 (hardcover : alk. paper)
 1. Copeland, Adam J., 1973--- Juvenile literature. 2. Wrestlers--United States--Biography--Juvenile
literature. I. Title.
 GV1196.C67S76 2011
 796.812092--dc22
 [B]   2011007193

This edition first published in 2012 by Bellwether Media, Inc.

Printed in the United States of America, North Mankato, MN.

080111   1187

CONTENTS

ROYAL RUMBLE......................4

WHO IS EDGE?.....................8

BECOMING A CHAMPION...14

GLOSSARY 22

TO LEARN MORE..................23

INDEX................................24

ROYAL RUMBLE

The 2010 World Wrestling Entertainment (WWE) **Royal Rumble** was nearing its end. It was an intense battle between 30 wrestlers. The last man standing would be the winner.

Shawn Michaels, Chris Jericho, and John Cena were in the ring when Edge joined the fight. He had missed the last seven months due to an injury. Some had thought he would never wrestle again.

BATISTA

Edge quickly hit Jericho with a move called the **Spear**. Then he pushed him out of the ring. Cena tried to slam Edge to the mat, but Edge **reversed** the move.

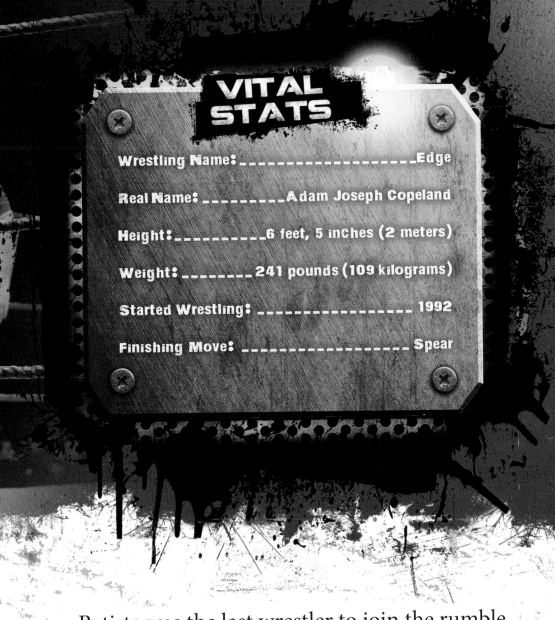

VITAL STATS

Wrestling Name: _ _ _ _ _ _ _ _ _ _ _ _ _ _ _ _ Edge

Real Name: _ _ _ _ _ _ _ _ _ Adam Joseph Copeland

Height: _ _ _ _ _ _ _ _ _ 6 feet, 5 inches (2 meters)

Weight: _ _ _ _ _ _ _ _ 241 pounds (109 kilograms)

Started Wrestling: _ _ _ _ _ _ _ _ _ _ _ _ _ _ _ _ 1992

Finishing Move: _ _ _ _ _ _ _ _ _ _ _ _ _ _ _ _ _ Spear

Batista was the last wrestler to join the rumble. Edge and Batista hurled Michaels out of the ring. Then Cena threw Batista over the ropes. Only two wrestlers were left. Cena charged at Edge, but Edge caught him and threw him out of the ring. Edge had won the Royal Rumble!

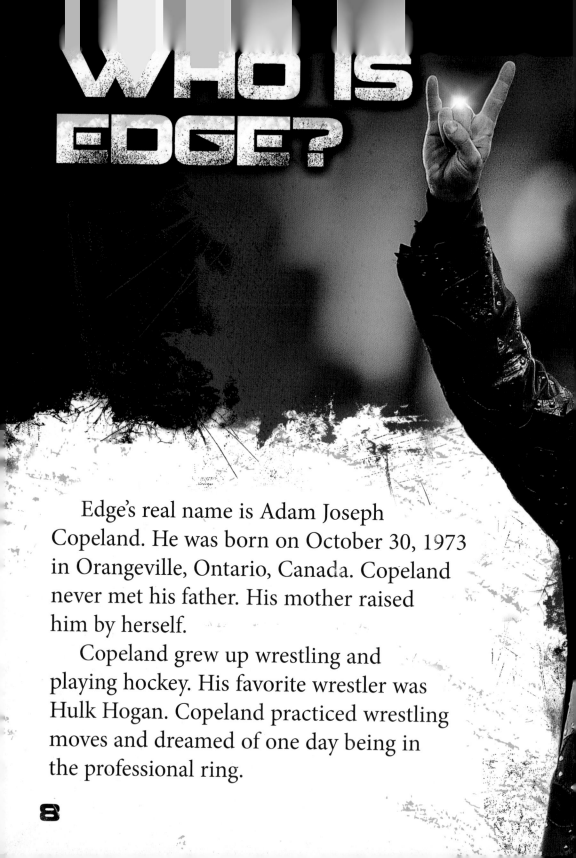

WHO IS EDGE?

Edge's real name is Adam Joseph Copeland. He was born on October 30, 1973 in Orangeville, Ontario, Canada. Copeland never met his father. His mother raised him by herself.

Copeland grew up wrestling and playing hockey. His favorite wrestler was Hulk Hogan. Copeland practiced wrestling moves and dreamed of one day being in the professional ring.

QUICK HIT!

Copeland and his friend Jason Reso started a wrestling group when they were teenagers. They named it the Getalong Gang. They worked out and wrestled together.

Copeland entered an essay contest when he was 18. He had to write about why he wanted to be a professional wrestler. First prize was a chance to train with professional wrestlers Ron Hutchison and Sweet Daddy Siki. Copeland won the contest.

Copeland went to Humber College in Toronto, Canada. He worked many jobs and trained in his free time. In 1992, he wrestled and lost his first professional match for a small league. He continued wrestling in small leagues over the next four years. In 1996, WWE star Bret Hart saw Copeland wrestle. He helped Copeland join WWE later that year.

BECOMING A CHAMPION

WWE wanted Copeland to train more. They sent him to Canada and Japan to wrestle in **house shows**. In 1998, he finally made his first WWE television appearance as Edge. He was a **heel** and joined a WWE group called the Ministry of Darkness.

JOHN CENA

QUICK HIT!

Edge won the WWE Intercontinental Championship in 1999. It was his first singles title.

Copeland first became famous for his tag team matches with Jason Reso. They wrestled as Edge and Christian. Together, they won seven WWE Tag Team Championships. However, the two wrestlers developed a **feud** and split up. Edge began wrestling in singles matches. In 2006, Edge beat John Cena for the WWE Championship. Over the next few years, Edge spent some time as a **face**. However, he was most often a heel. Fans loved to boo him.

Edge is a quick and powerful wrestler. He has several **signature moves**. In the one man con-chair-to, he crushes his opponent's head between two folding chairs. He performs the flapjack by tossing his opponent into the air and letting him crash down to the mat.

Edge's **finishing move** is the Spear. He charges and dives at his standing opponent. The impact drives the opponent hard into the mat. Few wrestlers can recover from this powerful move. It has helped Edge win many WWE championships and dominate in the ring.

GLOSSARY

face—a wrestler seen by fans as a hero

feud—a long-standing conflict between two people or teams

finishing move—a wrestling move meant to finish off an opponent so that he can be pinned

heel—a wrestler seen by fans as a villain

house shows—professional wrestling shows put on for live audiences; house shows are not shown on television.

reversed—turned the opponent's attack against him

Royal Rumble—a popular WWE battle between 30 wrestlers; instead of starting all at once, wrestlers join the battle every few minutes.

signature moves—moves that a wrestler is famous for performing

Spear—a move in which a wrestler charges and dives at a standing opponent, driving his shoulder into the opponent's stomach

TO LEARN MORE

AT THE LIBRARY

Black, Jake. *The Ultimate Guide to WWE.* New York, N.Y.: Grosset & Dunlap, 2010.

Kaelberer, Angie Peterson. *Cool Pro Wrestling Facts.* Mankato, Minn.: Capstone Press, 2011.

Nemeth, Jason D. *Edge.* Mankato, Minn.: Capstone Press, 2010.

ON THE WEB

Learning more about Edge
is as easy as 1, 2, 3.

1. Go to www.factsurfer.com.

2. Enter "Edge" into the search box.

3. Click the "Surf" button and you will see a list of related Web sites.

With factsurfer.com, finding more information is just a click away.

INDEX

Batista, 6, 7

Canada, 8, 12, 14

Cena, John, 4, 6, 7, 16, 17

face, 17

feud, 17

finishing move, 7, 20

flapjack, 19

Getalong Gang, 10

Hart, Bret, 12

heel, 14, 17

Hogan, Hulk, 8

house shows, 14

Humber College, 12

Hutchison, Ron, 11

Japan, 14

Jericho, Chris, 4, 6

Michaels, Shawn, 4, 7

Ministry of Darkness, 14

one man con-chair-to, 19

Reso, Jason, 10, 17

reversal, 6

Royal Rumble, 4, 7

signature moves, 19

Spear, 6, 7, 20

Sweet Daddy Siki, 11

training, 11, 12, 14

World Heavyweight
Championship, 19

World Wrestling Entertainment
(WWE), 4, 12, 14

WWE Championship, 17, 20

WWE Intercontinental
Championship, 16

WWE Tag Team
Championships, 17

The images in this book are reproduced through the courtesy of: Wire Image /
Getty Images, front cover, pp. 5, 11; Associated Press, pp. 4-5; Getty Images, pp.
6, 10, 14-15; AP Images for WWE, pp. 8-9, 12-13; Wire Image, pp. 16-17, 18-19;
Devin Chen, pp. 20-21.